THE POETIC ARCANA

A BOOK OF ORACLE POEMS

CONNOR BRYAN

First hardcover edition

Book design by Connor Bryan

ISBN 979-8-9864849-5-2

Published by Sun Cat Publishing

Dedicated to all the questions yet to be asked

Welcome

This book contains 52 poems, each with something to tell you. As oracle poems, you can pick a page number at random or flip through and stop on whatever page calls to you. Then, you can interpret the poem as you would an oracle or Tarot card.

I hope you enjoy this deck of pages, this book of cards, and I hope they bring you clarity and peace.

Love,

Connor ♡

Resurgence

come up again like smoke

and dip below what can be seen,

allowing your tides to turn

and the sweet embers of moonlight

to pass you by.

let yourself rest in this unknown

and leave them to wonder

when you'll be back.

Veil

the curtains draw back

and the soul is there,

frozen in time,

still smiling.

the music plays

and all along what was hidden

returns to the surface,

and what was seen

is shown in a new light.

Passage

you will not remember every step,

you will not savor every uneven path,

or count the dew drops in the clover at
your side.

but you will remember what each drop

has to teach you.

do not lose yourself in the details—

find yourself in the lessons.

Echo

it's staring back at you,

so similar but perhaps not

as you expected.

you tilt your head

and it tilts its own,

you let out a whisper,

it lets out a scream.

Vessel

open yourself to the light

and find the joy bursting

through your fingertips.

the light is already

within you.

you carry this spark,

and you light the fire.

Shiver

not all is well.

a shudder wracks

your bones,

and they would rattle

if not for the flesh

carefully tucked around them.

not all is as it seems,

but you have everything you need

within you.

Bloom

we only see

when flowers grow upwards,

reaching toward the sky.

we do not see

the ropes of roots

twisting through the soil,

surging toward sustenance.

we only celebrate the blossom,

but it takes work from within

to grow a single petal.

Mirage

it's in the distance

ahead of you

waving its hand languidly,

palm tree frond fingers

beckoning you closer.

but that's the problem

with finally arriving.

sometimes we see

what we want to see.

Junction

go to the right,

to what is right

for the heart that pounds

within your aching chest.

you know what is right.

close this book and

close your eyes and

remember—

you know what to do.

Hush

silence is not an absence.

it thrums, power surging through

your lips as you lift your words

to break it.

it is powerful to protect,

powerful to destroy.

the choice is yours.

Dreamscape

let yourself float

on thoughts big enough

to carry you away.

rise through the rubble

and see before you

a destiny, technicolor and heavy

with the possibilities you hold

carefully in your mind.

it is not a fault

to wonder.

it is not a flaw

to dream.

Whispers

something is not

as it seems,

but it seems exactly

as intended.

this smokescreen was built

just for you,

and these lies and half-truths

designed with you in mind.

now that you know,

look behind the curtain.

Fracture

it happened,

and it mattered.

life is now sorted

into befores

and afters.

it is okay to miss the path

you would have taken,

to grieve the you

you would have been.

grasp that version's hand

and walk forward.

Luster

does a pearl shine

within the darkness of the oyster?

or can it only glow so beautifully

once it's left its home

and the light floods in?

Reverie

breathe in.

fold your breath until it's small enough

and take it with you.

show it the sun,

the tides,

the rocky river bends,

the crows dancing.

when you are ready,

breathe out.

Forge

the urge is strong

pulsing in your chest,

burning like an aching fire.

create, create, create.

your perseverance is a kindness

to the world who will one day revel

in the light of your creation.

Pulse

the lifeblood you seek is not

where you're looking.

chances are, it's behind you,

lurking in your memory.

let your past fuel your present,

and stop looking for your own blood

inside someone else's heart.

Equinox

balance is key

in all things.

the sun does not set

without the moon to follow.

when it rains,

the earth drinks deeply

but doesn't drown.

find the balance,

find the key.

Unraveling

these threads wind tightly

around your fingers,

urging you not to forget.

pluck the end and untie the bow,

and allow yourself

to remember.

then allow yourself to let go.

Kindling

do you feel it? smoldering

beneath the soil you once trod?

the sparks you let fly

so long ago

are catching, glowing beneath the surface.

your warmest nights are upon you,

a fire set by days past.

Trace

if the road is unclear ahead,

turn around

but do not turn back.

look to the steps you left

and remind yourself the reason

you left them.

suddenly, the path

is simpler to follow

because the road behind

is a winding reminder.

Drift

you would not beg a leaf

to fall faster,

would not wish the winter

would rob the trees

of their color any sooner.

if your heart seeks to float

on the air like the snow,

you may let it.

there is no view more beautiful

and no feeling more divine.

Ember

you glow and shift and dance,

a shining speck of sun

in the dark of the night.

some would burn out,

spin into smoke,

but touch the right tree,

land in the right leaves,

and you can ignite.

Tide

give the shift a chance

to settle in your soul.

let the change dance

in your bones

until the fear turns

to hope.

newness is frightening,

but it's also life itself.

every fresh day,

every first meeting,

every opportunity

to wash in with the waves,

and out to the ocean.

the newness is coming.

be ready to float.

Threshold

the door floats

suspended in air

waiting for your steps

to unlock it.

this entry was made for you,

has been waiting for the day

you'd discover its key

was within your hand all along.

unlock the door

and walk through.

Haven

it is okay to grieve

the safety you once felt.

it is okay to mourn

the way this place once was.

but do not lose yourself

in these thoughts.

do not ignore the pathways away

toward true safety.

do not leave yourself in harm's way

for the sake of a memory.

find your new safe haven,

and leave this place

tucked safely in your mind.

Murmur

do you hear it?

the way everything sings,

the way the world hums

as it turns,

dancing in the darkness

of the universe.

listen to its signs.

you'll soon find

no melody is meaningless.

Nest

the wanderer parts

with her home,

setting out in search

of the world.

she does not consider

those she leaves behind,

but they do not consider

what she'll one day find.

Compass

you are going

the direction your blood

wants to pump,

following the way

your bones rattle.

listen to your soul,

the way it sings louder

the closer you get.

you know the way.

Tether

you have permission

to remove these heirlooms

that feel like manacles,

to find your own way

through the trees.

you can cut the cord

pulling you back.

Serendipity

what a sign!

what a life

that would pull you toward

this moment.

what a beautiful coincidence,

a lovely happenstance

that led you here.

it all converges,

and it is all meant to be.

Prism

the energy you receive

splits within you,

refracts into brilliance.

let it pour forth,

painting the sky

with colors you've never seen.

it is okay to let go

of what you've been given.

don't keep this light

locked inside.

Remnant

it may feel

like nothing is left

of the way things were,

but you are made

of everyone you've ever loved

and everyone you've ever lost.

when you look into a mirror,

you are seeing countless souls.

close your eyes.

the past is within you.

Chasm

the canyon is wide,

and the fall would be far.

the only way through

is across,

but the only way across

is with help.

do not be afraid to call out

across the distance.

Tapestry

we are threads

carefully weaving together

lives and knowledge and beings

until our strings intertwine

and we are one image,

ornate and beautiful.

Root

send yourself downward,

search within.

the answers you seek

are tucked away

where the sun can't see it,

where the rain can't find it.

it's where we begin,

and where we end.

Flux

the change is the steadiness,

the only thing we can count on.

the sun will set each evening

but it will paint the sky

with different colors,

the clouds rolling in different ways.

the change is the only constant

and in that way

it can be a comfort.

Talisman

carry this feeling with you

so that you may remember

what it was like

to cross these waters,

to weather this storm.

keep it tucked in your pocket,

a memory you hold close

to remember you've come far.

Resolve

your passion, wit, and want

will start the fire that lights the candle.

doors will open for you,

but only if you turn the handle.

Liminal

sometimes these lights flicker

and you wonder if this place is real

or if your mind has wandered farther

than you meant it.

sometimes this place looks

both familiar and foreign,

like your name spoken

in another tongue.

Sanctuary

find safety not in the steeple

but in the people.

the love comes from within you,

not without you.

hold the hand of your neighbor

and never let go

of what brings us together.

remember that you are a piece

of a whole.

Glimmer

the night sky is dark,

or so we assume.

but if we truly look,

we'll see lights

that aren't visible in the day.

sometimes the brightness

drowns out its own light.

take these moments

here in the dark

to savor the glow of the stars.

Horizon

it dares you to find it,

begs you to cross it,

gives you a reason to row.

though the earth is round,

and you'll never find it,

the journey is worth the risk.

Silhouette

she dances in shadow,

light wrapping around her edges

as she hides secret after secret

within her twirls.

do not trust everything

she tells you,

but do not fear

a bit of half-truth.

Essence

the ghost of you is still beautiful,

even without your spark.

it's still you,

even when you're floating through

the days like a spirit.

don't be afraid to don a sheet

and haunt your home for a while.

Lantern

the light you need

is in your hand.

seek it out

and see.

Tremor

though your hands may shake,

this fear is not a hindrance,

this fright is not a detriment,

but a reminder to stand firm

and push through.

you may be afraid,

but that is proof that it matters.

Oasis

it is not something you find,

but something you recognize

in the flowers you planted,

in the home that you made,

in the laughter that floats

from the other room.

the perfection is found

in the commonplace,

the beauty in the everyday.

Fable

take the words you read

as allegory,

a warning sign,

not just a story.

the hardships and triumphs

you find in the pages

will guide you toward

the perfect changes.

Mosaic

you are a mix

of everything you've ever loved,

all of their chips and pieces

combining into a pattern

that creates you,

even those you wish

to forget.

they changed you, yes,

but for the better

and your image

will continue to grow forever.

Descent

the spiral staircase

digs deep

into the parts of you

you wish to conceal

but the shadows that lurk there

are only dark

because they have not seen light.

walk down the steps

and face them with compassion.

they are parts of you after all.

Repose

rest now,

and dream of the days

you miss most.

they will guide you into the future.

but for now, bathe in the memories,

and allow yourself the time to be slow,

the space to be gentle.

About the Author

Connor Bryan is a poet and fiction author from Florida. Find out more about her work at connorbryanwrites.com and keep in touch on Instagram and TikTok at @prettyquickpoetry.

Also by Connor Bryan:

Jack Finch Believes in Ghosts

The Reprise

Give Me a Word: 150 Poems for Strangers

Milton Keynes UK
Ingram Content Group UK Ltd.
UKHW021450161124
451187UK00004B/27